Lisa Dozier

BOARD AF

Text and images © 2021 by Lisa Dozier

Published by Artes Gráficas Palermo Madrid, Spain
c/o 115 West 45th Street, Suite 603, New York,
NY 10036. www.boardaf.com

ISBN: 978-0-578-31660-4

Library of Congress Control Number: 2021923260

Photography & Text:
Lisa Dozier

Cover & Interior Design:
Manuel González Ruiz
MAGOATELIER.COM

Printed in Spain

This book is dedicated
to my mini muses:
Maddy, my sun
Colton, my moon
Emmy, my stars

Dear Reader,
~~~~~~~

Board AF was born of a chaotic concoction of work burnout, pandemic coping and, most of all, connecting with my children. My career has always been a key identifier in my life, because it has been my passion since the fourth grade. In March of 2020, I had clocked almost 125,000 miles in the sky over the previous year with my theatrical management company. Suddenly, because of the pandemic, the theatre industry was on indefinite intermission.

I woke up and realized that while I was out earning the dough, my kids had regressed in their eating to chicken nuggets, hot dogs, and frozen pizza. Their once adventurous foodie spirits had morphed into favoring ketchup as their core food group.

I spent hours in the kitchen poring over meticulous French sauces, duck, noodles... and my kids looked at the plates and still asked for ketchup. One Saturday morning early in the pandemic, I got an idea and pulled out the walnut cutting board that I have used the heck out of over the years. Nothing fancy. I lined the kitchen counter with fruit of all

sorts, made dipping sauces, and then stacked up kid-sized pancakes. I put on music and arranged it all on the cutting board and set it in front of my kids at the table.

"What do we do with this, mommy?"
they asked. I told them to go for it and line their plates with whatever they wanted from the board. They were hooked.

We migrated from pancakes to duck tonkotsu ramen, lamb shanks braised in red wine, fried green tomatoes, and fish & chips. They gobbled it all up, game to try anything, happily picking away at each board's ingredients. It was more than food—it was a way to remind my kids that, amidst all of the uncertainty, they are safe and loved. And that there is joy to be found in the everyday.

Filling my time with this hobby became my retreat—a source of joy every single day. I hope it gives you some joy too!

xo

Lisa

Photography by: **Russ Rowland**

TABLE OF CONTENTS

BOARDS

- Pancake
- Make-Your-Own Breakfast Sandwich
- Donut
- Cinnamon Roll
- Egg
- French Toast
- Bagels & Schmear
- Muffin Pancake
- Yogurt Parfait Fruit
- Rainbow Breakfast

~1~

Break-
fast

Board Chapter

PANCAKE BOARD

(SERVES 6-8)

Pancakes– where it all started. My kiddos love Saturday morning pancakes. So much so, that sometimes I wait to tell them until the morning of because my itty bitties will wake up extra early that morning if they know! I wanted them to enjoy their maple syrup, but also get some fruit in their tummies with it. Then, the pancake board was born.

ON THE BOARD:

- 10-15 pancakes
- 2 bananas, sliced
- 1 cup blueberries
- 1 cup raspberries
- 1-2 cups strawberries
- 10-12 strips of bacon *(BACON!)*
- ¼ cup semisweet chocolate chips
- 3 tbsp butter
- ½ cup maple syrup *(the good kind)*
- ½ cup homemade berry jam

PANCAKE MIX RECIPE:

- 3 cups all purpose flour
- 1 tsp baking soda
- 2 ½ tsp baking powder
- ½ tbsp kosher salt
- 2 tbsp sugar

When ready to make, combine mix, 2 cups whole milk, 1 tbsp lemon juice, 2 whisked eggs and cook on griddle. Flip when you see bubbles.

TIP:
This pancake mix makes an awesome gift around the holidays in mason jars, and keeps for about 4 months.

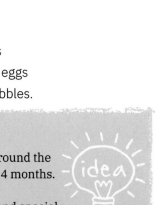

VARIATIONS ON A THEME: For birthdays and special occasions, we are big fans of one-of-a-kind pancakes.

MAKE-YOUR-OWN BREAKFAST SANDWICH BOARD (SERVES 8-10)

When I first moved to New York City in 2003, I had no idea how to cook. Once, I set fire to a dish towel trying to fry an egg. When I decided that it was time to crack that nut (yup, pun intended), I spent weekend mornings with a pot of coffee, a notebook, and cooking shows. I'd handwrite the recipes flashed up on the screen, attempting to scribble down every ingredient and tip. Ina Garten, Lydia Bastianich, the team at America's Test Kitchen; all of them became friendly faces, cheering me on to conquer the castle of my own kitchen.

Boiling pasta turned into slow simmering Bolognese. Grilled cheese transformed into croque madames. I began a journey of local farmers markets and started a supper club each month. I created a secret Facebook group where I would post the menu based on the farmers market fare and recipes from the greats, and the first 12 to sign up would be the guest list. Often, those who came didn't know anyone else attending. Ah, those dinners would go on well into the night, full of feasting and conversation.

Discovering Ina Garten's waffle iron hash browns during the pandemic ignited the same feelings from that time period in me, a flurry of inspiration. Thinking of how I could take such a clever recipe and turn it into a board, I realized that the interactive component of making one's own sandwich with other farmers market ingredients would be a blast. It has since become a weekend morning staple in our house, just like Ina's show was to me all those years ago!

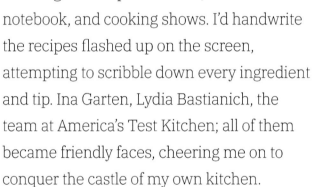

ON THE BOARD

- 10-12 traditional or hash brown waffles
- 1 package, thick cut bacon *(BACON!)*
- 2 large sliced beefsteak tomatoes
- 6-8 fried eggs *(with yolk still runny)*
- 10 Provolone cheese slices
- 1 large bunch grapes or other fruit as a side, fill board as needed

TIP:
Fry the eggs last! Keep the hash brown waffles in the oven at 250 degrees while you make the eggs. Then everything is warm for serving.

DONUT BOARD

(SERVES 6-8)

Donuts are one of my kids' most favorite breakfast dishes on the weekend. As they stumble out of bed in the morning, I love watching their faces light up upon being told donuts are on the menu.

We garnish with seasonal fruit, especially berries, so the kiddos get their fill of good-for-you ingredients to go with all the sugar.

CAKE DONUT RECIPE:

The best thing about cake donuts? They are shockingly easy! (shhhh... don't tell anyone!) Here is our guide to super duper easy cake donuts, which you can customize with toppings from your pantry.

- 3 cups all purpose flour
- 1 tsp baking soda
- 2 ½ tsp baking powder
- ½ tbsp kosher salt
- 2 tbsp sugar
- ¼ cup ingredient of your choice
  (jam, chocolate, you pick!)

Preheat oven to 350 degrees. Grease two six-hole donut pans. Whisk all ingredients together so there are no lumps. Batter should be a thicker consistency than pancakes. Spoon batter into donut pans until half full. Bake for 12-14 minutes until toothpick comes out clean. Once out of the oven, you can dip in melted chocolate, sugar glaze, or eat as is.

CINNAMON ROLL BOARD

(SERVES 10-12)

ON THE BOARD:

- 1 batch cinnamon rolls
- 6 hard-boiled eggs, sliced in half
  (topped with parsley and a sprinkle of salt)
- 10-12 slices bacon *(BACON!)*
- 3 cups fresh fruit
- Seeds of 1 pomegranate
- 1 lemon, wedged

PRESENTATION TIP:
Lay out a board's worth of cinnamon rolls in a fun pattern and line up the fruit, bacon, and eggs around them. Replenish rolls as needed.

An anchor tradition in our house is cinnamon rolls every Christmas morning. We make them from scratch the night before, and then pop 'em in the oven first thing when we wake, so we can smell them baking away while the kids open their presents under the tree. We devour them accompanied by bacon, eggs, and assorted berries. My son Colton and I love to top our rolls with pomegranate seeds for crunch.

EGG BOARDS

(SERVES 6-8)

If stuck on a deserted island, which food would I choose? That's easy—eggs!. A savory sunny-side up egg topped with scallions and parsley is my ultimate breakfast go-to staple. We do a lot of boards that highlight all glorious things that are the egg. Fried, scrambled, poached—you name it, we have crushed it. Here are some of our all-time fave eggspirations.

BACON EGG CUPS

We often make easy bacon egg cups for our boards. Place muffin tin upside down on a baking sheet. Spray heavily with oil or butter to grease. Wrap a bacon piece around each muffin holder, overlapping the ends so they fuse together when cooking. Bake at 400 degrees for 15-18 minutes. Fill with scrambled eggs or, as shown here, eggs cooked in greased muffin tins, turned the right way up, for 15-18 minutes at 350 degrees.

TOAD IN A HOLE

We prefer challah or thick country bread for these. Using a dough cutter or circle cookie cutter, cut out a hole in the center of the bread. Butter both sides of bread and place on hot skillet, medium heat. Crack eggs, keeping yolks whole, in center hole until egg whites are cooked through. Sprinkle grated cheese on top of bread while cooking. Top with Kosher salt and parsley.

FRENCH TOAST BOARD

(SERVES 6-8)

French toast, to me, is the pièce de résistance of the breakfast experience. The right balance of sweet and salty. On Mondays, the kids and I make our bread for the week. By the time the weekend rolls around, the loaf has gotten slightly crunchy to be the right consistency for the ultimate French toast. We slice the bread extra thick and cut in half for peak surface-level flavor.

ON THE BOARD:

- 12-15 pieces French toast
- 2 cups blueberries
- 2 peaches, sliced
- 1 cup cherries
- 1-2 cups strawberries
- 1 lemon, wedged and sliced
- ½ cup maple syrup
- 4 tbsp butter

FRENCH TOAST RECIPE:

- 1 loaf challah bread, ideally 3-4 days old
- 3 eggs
- 4 cups milk *(whole)*
- ¼ cup brown sugar
- 2 tbsp cinnamon
- 1 tbsp vanilla
- Pinch of salt
- 2 tbsp unsalted butter

Slice challah in 1-inch pieces, set aside. Combine all other ingredients except butter. Pour half of mixture in a large, shallow pan. Set bread pieces on top. Pour remaining liquid mixture on top. Heat grill pan and butter. Grill french toast 2-3 minutes on each side, until golden brown.

TIP:
Make sure to let the French toast pieces soak in the eggs for 15 minutes so you get that right texture, and only use butter for the pan to get that golden brown hue.

idea

BAGELS & SCHMEAR BOARD

(SERVES 6-8)

Hailing from New York City, our family loves a weekend bagel breakfast. Here is a spread from Emmy's 5th birthday; she devoured that rainbow bagel! We make sure to keep plenty of bagels on the side to replenish the board as needed, as well as have everyone's top picks of schmears readily available.

MUFFIN PANCAKE BERRY BOARD

(SERVES 6-8)

 e love doing muffin and pancake boards when we have guests staying with us for their last day. That way, those who are able to stay can line their plates with pancakes, syrup, and all the fruit. Those who have to head out can have their pick of muffins and fruit to take on the go.

YOGURT PARFAIT FRUIT BOARD

(SERVES 6-8)

This board was inspired by all things summer and wanting to give the kids a sweet, healthy treat. Maddy, my oldest, and I made the granola cups the night before and let them dry overnight. We arranged the fruit to encapsulate the colors of a summer sunset on the beach.

ON THE BOARD:

- 2 granola yogurt cups per person
- 2 cups pineapple
- 2 oranges, peeled and sliced
- 2 cups seedless diced watermelon
- 2 cups strawberries

GRANOLA CUPS RECIPE:

Combine 1 ½ cups rolled oats, 1 ½ tsp cinnamon, 1 tsp kosher salt. Press into sprayed muffin tins and form into cups by hand. Bake in pre-heated 350 degree oven for 15 minutes. Let cool, then pop out of tins. They may still be fragile. Let sit for at minimum 30 minutes or overnight. Before serving, combine 2 ½ cups vanilla yogurt and 3 tbsp honey. Then spoon yogurt mixture into cups.

PRESENTATION TIP:
Maddy and I had fun doing the blueberries and stars on this one, but we have also done these where the kids can decorate their own before eating.

RAINBOW BREAKFAST BOARD

(SERVES 6-8)

Breakfast rainbow treats are a staple in our house for every child's birthday morning. Pancakes, donuts, waffles... you name it, we have rainbowfied it! This tradition has become such joy for us that even adults get rainbow birthday boards.

ON THE BOARD:

- 10-12 Rainbow Pancakes
  (see presentation tip)
- 1 cup blueberries
- 1 cup raspberries
- ½ cup whipped cream
  (rainbow sprinkle topped, of course!)
- 2 bananas, sliced
- ½ cup chocolate chips
  (ideally rainbow, if you can find)

RAINBOW CAKE DONUTS RECIPE:
(Adaption of cake donut recipe on page 15)

Mix donut batter, pour ¼ cup portions of batter into five different bowls. Place the following amounts of food coloring in the respective bowls on top of batter, and stir in until even:

- Bowl 1: 3 drops blue
- Bowl 2: 2 drops red (we like ours to be on the pink side as pink is Emmy's favorite color!)
- Bowl 3: 3 drops yellow
- Bowl 4: 3 drops green
- Bowl 5: 2 drops blue + 2 drops red

Spoon one tablespoon from each of the five bowls into the donut molds. You can leave as is, or run a toothpick gently through the batter once all poured for a swirl effect. Bake at 350 degrees for 12-14 minutes. Do not overbake as it will dilute the rainbow hues.

PRESENTATION TIP:
For the rainbow pancakes, we recommend a white flour pancake mix. Once the pancakes start to bubble, cover with regular rainbow sprinkles and rainbow sparkling sugar sprinkles for the shimmer/3D rainbow effect before flipping. The kids LOVE being the designated sprinkle pourer, and the birthday kid always gets the honors!

BOARDS

- Champagne Batter Fish & Chips
- Lobstah (Roll)
- Ramen
- Taco Tuesday
- Burger
- Grill
- Sushi
- Ballpark
- Flatbread

Dinner

Board Chapter

CHAMPAGNE BATTER FISH & CHIPS BOARD

(SERVES 6-8)

I am a theatre producer, and I was lucky enough to have a musical in London which brought me from NYC across the Atlantic two times a month for a year. Oh, London, how I adore you. There is no city I love getting lost in more than you. Wandering the cobblestone streets, having a cuppa, and then making my way around the neighborhoods sampling British staples. The top of that being fish & chips.

When Covid hit and all theatre and borders were shuttered between the two countries, I missed London deeply. This board was done early on during the quarantine period. It is a love letter to my city away from home.

ON THE BOARD:

- 1 fried fish fillet per person (*I prefer cod for this*)
- 3 cups peas (*I only put one cup on the board and replenish as needed*)
- ¼ cup malt vinegar
- 1 lemon, wedged
- ¼ cup Dijon mustard
- ¼ cup whole grain mustard
- 1 cup homemade tartar sauce (*recipe below*)
- Parsley garnish

TARTAR SAUCE RECIPE:

- 1 cup fresh mayo
- ½ cup diced pickles
- ¼ cup finely chopped parsley
- 2 tbsp lemon juice
- 1 tsp Worcestershire sauce
- Kosher salt to taste

Combine all ingredients. Top with diced parsley once on board for color.

TIP:
Whisk 1 cup of freshly popped champagne or prosecco into your batter for an airy freshness to the fish fry. I recommend using only bubbly you would drink—both for taste in the batter and so the rest of the bottle does not go to waste!
BONUS TIP: Always, always, always double fry your French fries. It is crucial for the right balance of crunch and color!

LOBSTAH (ROLL) BOARD

(SERVES 6-8)

ON THE BOARD:

- 3 lobster rolls, cut in half *(served Maine style)*
- 1 whole lobster
- 1 lb stone crab claws *(pre-cracked)*
- ½ lb shrimp, seasoned with Old Bay
- 6-8 ears corn on the cob, cut in half
- 1 cup mustard dip
- ½ cup butter
- 1 lemon, wedged

MUSTARD DIP RECIPE:

- 1 egg yolk
- 1 tbsp whole grain mustard
- 1 ½ tsp fresh lemon juice
- 1 ½ tsp Kosher salt
- 1 tsp water
- ¾ cup olive oil
- 1 tsp Worcestershire sauce

In a standing mixer or by hand, whisk together egg yolk, lemon, mustard, salt, and water. Slowly incorporate oil in a thin stream while whisking so it emulsifies. Stir in Worcestershire. Once completely combined, taste for salt as needed. Chopped parsley can be added.

Anyone who knows me knows that I LOVE seafood. If it came outta the ocean, I will happily put it in my mouth. This board was inspired by a few places near and dear to my heart that focus on all things under the sea, as well as the desire to make them at home for the kiddos to try.

First, the center of this board is the lobster (as it should be!), influenced by Luke's Lobster that started in the East Village in my hometown of New York City. Luke's serves only sustainable and traceable seafood, and now ships around the country! I used cooked frozen lobster meat from the grocery store and stuffed it in homemade hoagie rolls. Once the lobster meat was in the rolls, I drizzled the lobster with melted butter.

Second, stone crab season runs October-May. I lived in Miami for many years, and Joe's Stone Crab was always a highlight to take visiting friends and family. My homemade mustard dip is a nod to those sweet crustacean times and Joe's famous mustard sauce.

PRESENTATION TIP:
The primary colors of this board are red and yellow. To make the lobster pop, layer the whole lobster on top of the rolls at the very end of arranging. Make sure to have crackers on hand for the whole lobster!

RAMEN BOARD

Two years ago, I had the most wonderous adventure getting to travel to Tokyo. I devoured ramen, the classic Japanese noodle soup that originated in China, in as many varieties as I could get a spoon in. There are a million reasons to love this dish. The broth, the protein, the noodles! Ramen's rich and soulful qualities make the comfort of eating it a magical and transformative experience. I wanted to share a piece of this with my family, who now all love ramen as much as me!

ON THE BOARD:

- 4-6 soft boiled duck eggs
- 1 cup Kimchi
- Baby bok choi *(1 piece per person)*
- Duck or chicken breast, sliced
- Pork belly *(1 slice per person)*
- 1 cup shiitaki mushrooms
- 1 cup lemongrass
- ½ cup bean sprouts
- 2 cups duck or chicken stock per person
- Ramen noodles, prepared
- Shoyu Tare

SHOYU TARE RECIPE:

Whisk together 1 cup soy sauce, ½ cup mirin, 1 tsp rice wine vinegar, 1 tsp sesame oil, 1 tsp sugar, 1 tsp fresh grated ginger, and 2 small minced cloves of garlic over low heat. I make this the day before.

PRESENTATION TIP:

When serving this, I set individual bowls down with 2 cups of stock, 2 tbsp of the shoyu tare sauce, and noodles. Then, everyone individually fills their bowls with the remaining ingredients from the board, placed in the middle of the table, as their hearts desire.

idea

TACO TUESDAY BOARD

(SERVES 6-8)

In our house, we live for TACO NIGHT! The little ones love the independence of helping themselves to make their own tacos, and the adults love the variety of ingredients.

Taco night does not commence until we sing along to our own anthem of "It's Raining Tacos." Cheese refrain, anyone?

Maddy's favorite part of taco night is making her "family famous" guacamole. 10 year old made, tested, and approved. Recipe below.

ON THE BOARD:

- 1 cup salsa
- 2 cups Maddy's guac *(recipe below)*
- 1 cup sour cream or plain Greek yogurt
- ½ cup diced or sliced cherry tomatoes
- 2 cups cheese cheese cheese cheese
- ¼ cup sliced Jalapeños
- 2 cups roasted mini peppers
- 1 lime, wedged
- Cilantro garnish

MADDY'S GUAC RECIPE:

- 4 mashed avocados
- ¼ cup diced fresh tomatoes
- ½ tbsp fresh squeezed lemon juice
- Kosher salt to taste
- 1 clove garlic, finely minced
- 1 tbsp olive oil

Combine all ingredients. Eat!

TIP:
To keep taco night fresh, we love to mix up the proteins from week to week. Ground beef, shredded chicken, shrimp—you name it, we have taco-ed it!

idea

BURGER BOARD

(SERVES 4-6)

Burgers are a food group in our household. Sometimes we mix it up with different themes, but the consistency of getting to put your burger together, the way YOU want it, at the table always gives a spice of excitement for a weekday meal. Whether it is the dog days of summer, or you are bundling up during the winter months, we think burgers are a year-round comfort meal.

ON THE BOARD:

- 10-12 rolls
- 2 large tomatoes, sliced
- 4 slices cheese of your choosing, we prefer Provolone!
- 1 cup shredded romaine lettuce
- 2 avocados, sliced
- Pickle spears
- Red onion slices
- Condiments of your preference

BASIL PESTO SPREAD RECIPE:

- 2 ½ cups shredded basil leaves
- ¼ cup unshelled sunflower seeds
  (*our spin substitute on the regular pine nuts. Cheaper swap too!*)
- ½ cup olive oil (*regular or extra virgin will do*)
- ¾ cup fresh grated Parmigiano Reggiano cheese
- 2 cloves garlic
- Salt to taste

In a food processor or mini chopper, pulse olive oil, sunflower seeds, and garlic. Add basil leaves, cheese, and salt. Pulse until blended. Fab for burgers, pasta, and seafood!

PRESENTATION TIP:
For our burger boards, we like to do sliders so we can fit more ingredients on the board and replenish as necessary. Also, aren't mini burgers the cutest?!

idea

GRILL BOARD

(SERVES 4-6)

Few things give us as much satisfaction as seeing that char grill texture on one of our ingredients (and then getting to eat it!). Our family enjoys summer days of grill-only dinner items, like this board. We raid the farmers market and then our fridge to see what can be grilled. As a result, every grill board is an adventure!

SUSHI BOARD

(SERVES 8-10)

Maddy, 10, and I love the process of creating sushi rolls together. From trips to our local H Mart for the freshest sushi grade toro and salmon, to researching new ingredients, to the calming act of making and raking the rice, we enjoy every part. However, devouring them is simply the best!

BALLPARK BOARD

(SERVES 4-6)

There are few things our family loves more in this world than wings and hot dogs. Put them together and you have a dream team for a winning dinner! Perfect for all the sports in our house, we make this board while watching baseball in the spring (go Yankees!) or football Sundays during the fall (go Bills!). Every time, it is a home run... or a touch down. Goal!!!

ON THE BOARD:

- 1 lb wings
- 1 package Nathan's hot dogs
  (*the Coney Island way!*)
- 1 package hot dog buns, toasted
- 1 cup celery sticks
- 1 cup baby or sliced carrots
- 4 cups chips, fries or tots (*whatever you fancy*)
- Condiments of your desire, in small serving bowls

MIDFIELD WING SEASONING RECIPE:

- ½ cup Kosher salt
- 3 tbsp paprika
- 3 tbsp garlic powder
- 1 tbsp fresh ground black pepper

Preheat oven to 425 degrees. Toss all ingredients together, then coat wings in seasoning. On a greased or parchment lined baking tray, place the wings on a single layer where they aren't touching. Bake for 35 minutes, flipping them over halfway through, until juices run clear.

FLATBREAD BOARDS

We love making bread in our home and decorating it for all the occasions. Here are some of our greatest hits displayed on our board.

We prefer to use a focaccia-style base for our flatbread extravaganzas. Combine one packet dry yeast with 2 ½ cups tepid water until foamy (5-8 minutes). Combine with 4 cups all purpose flour, 1 cup bread flour, ¼ cup Kosher salt. Combine with ¼ cup extra virgin olive oil and place in a large covered mixing bowl. Let rise for 4-6 hours until it more than doubles in size. Press into a large greased baking sheet and poke holes all over dough with your fingers. Let rise for an additional hour, then decorate! Bake at 375 degrees for 35 minutes or until golden brown.

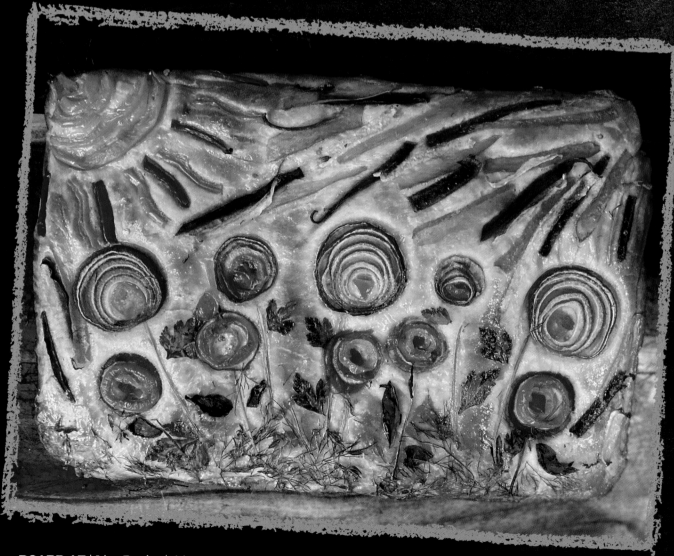

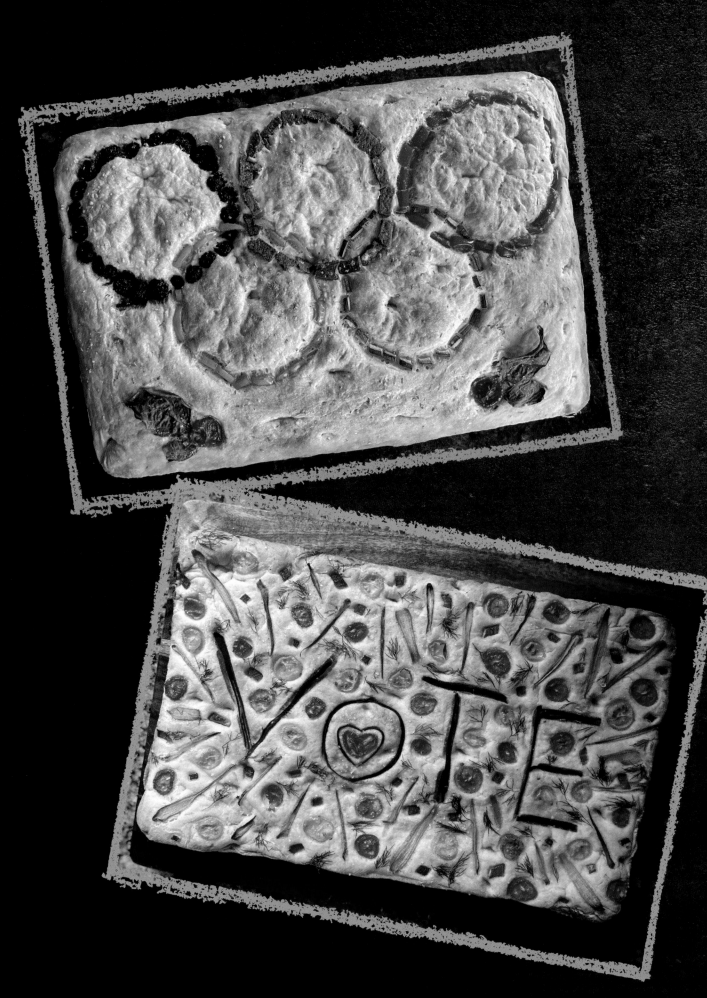

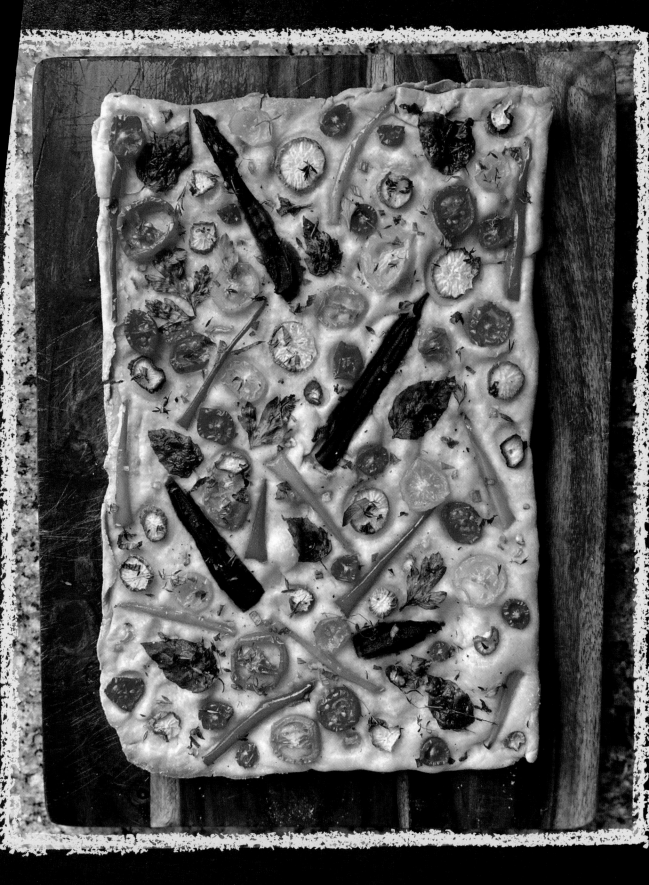

BOARDS

- Fruit Mosaic
- Hot Cocoa
- Slumber Party
- Mini Fruit Pies
- Ice Cream Sundae
- Funnel Cake

Dessert
Board Chapter

FRUIT MOSAIC BOARDS

A few weeks before writing this, I was in the tiny kitchen of my apartment– sitting on the kids' step stool, coffee in hand, watching the clothes spin in the dryer. The kids were going off the wall, and I was trying to find a small moment of solitude. It didn't work. "MOMMY! WHERE ARE YOU????" On and on.

They needed to eat, and I needed to get some energy. Emmy, my youngest, wandered in and asked to help. I said to her "Let's make something beautiful." We pulled out all of the fruit and stared at it. She washed the berries then handed them to me while stealing some along the way.

On days like that day, I find my happiness (and sanity!) in taking something that is ubiquitous and transforming it so we can appreciate its beauty.

HOW TO:

METHOD 1: Take a food-safe paper such as parchment and cut a piece to the size of your board. Using a food-safe pen, sketch an outline of your design to have lines as your guide.
Set page on your board and cover with fruit, following the lines on your sketch.

METHOD 2: Freestyle it. This is my favorite way to create because it is always a colorful surprise to how it turns out!

SLUMBER PARTY BOARD

M y kiddos love slumber parties. During pandemic shelter-in days, we had countless sleepovers to make the time feel more special. Movies and candy and pillow fights... oh my!

MINI FRUIT PIES BOARD

Nothing says summer more to us than berry pie, and we love every type! The joy of these little pies lies in the intricate decorations made with dough stamps that can be purchased at any kitchen store. We like to make three different fillings and leave it to mystery as to which pie is which flavor!

HOT COCOA BOARD

(SERVES 6-8)

Every year, we have a Polar Express night around the holidays. We read the book and simulate boarding the train to watch the movie. Hot cocoa is a requirement. Bonuses for this board are little kitchen time, advance prep, and perfect for tiny guests!

I gather the sweet treats and arrange them on a bed of green and red glitter sprinkles. Chocolate covered pretzels, candy canes, and marshmallows are topped with festive red licorice bows, making this board a gift for kids of all ages.

ON THE BOARD:

- 1 cup hot cocoa mix (*I mix this with the red glitter sprinkles once in the bowl.*)
- 2 cups marshmallows, all sorts
- 1 pack twizzlers
- 1 pack chocolate squares
- 1 cup white chocolate kisses
- 1 cup chocolate covered pretzels for a salty contrast
- Red and green candies (*red and green chocolate candies, chocolate balls, anything cool to fill the board*)

CHOCOLATE SPOONS RECIPE:

A tradition with this board is the homemade chocolate stirring spoons. And they are SO EASY to make! Molds can be purchased online or at a craft store.

Melt white chocolate according to package directions and pour into molds. Then, melt a small amount of red melting chocolate and dip a toothpick in the red. Take the toothpick and swirl into the white chocolate in the mold. Less is better to keep the marbling aesthetic in tact.

Let cool for 1-2 hours in the fridge, then pop out of the mold! These can be made days ahead of time too.

ICE CREAM

(SERVES 8-10)

SUNDAE BOARD

Sundays are for Sundaes, amiright? We love a customizable ice cream board experience for a special treat. My favorite part is hitting up our favorite local ice cream shops to pick our flavors. Each child gets to pick one topping for the board.

FUNNEL CAKE BOARD

(SERVES 4-6)

This board evokes memories of trips to the state fair. Perfect for a dessert treat or decadent brunch, having a variety of fruit to accompany the funnel cake makes the board a universal pick for both the sweet tooth holders and health conscious members of your fam.

BOARDS
- Harvest Fall for 2
- Hometown Favorites Traditional
- Mom Comes to Visit
- Spring Veggie

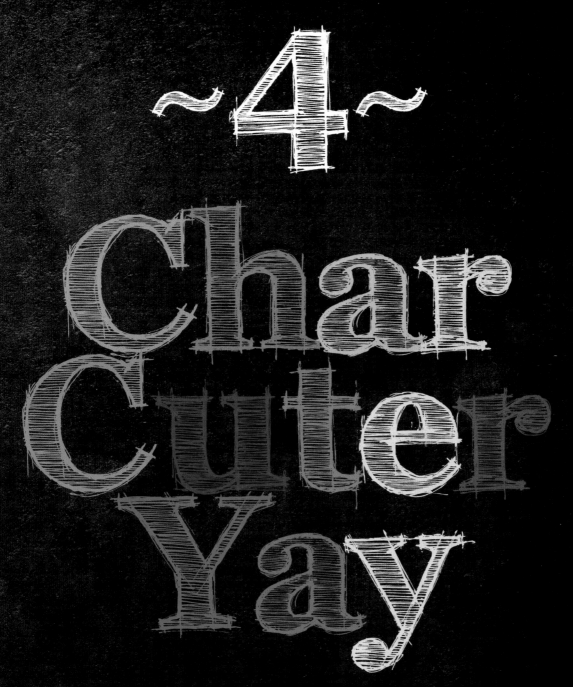

~4~
Char Cuter Yay

Board Chapter

HARVEST FALL
FOR 2 BOARD

(SERVES 2, THOUGH WOULD ALSO WORK FOR 3-4 TO GRAZE)

While I love making boards for a crowd, I find such joy in the connection of sitting back and enjoying a board for two. The conversation lends itself to the inherent storytelling that comes when sharing the journey of picking items for the board. This board is filled with the bounty of the Hudson Valley in my home state of New York, topped with decadent cheeses, meats, and treats from our favorite neighborhood shop, Hiller & Moon in Brooklyn.

HOMETOWN FAVORITES TRADITIONAL BOARD

(SERVES 3-4)

When curating a traditional charcuterie board, one of the most enjoyable parts of the process is picking items from local businesses to put on that board that I know friends and family will find special. I start with where everything should stem from – where the cheese should go, and fill in around. This board has cheeses from Cheese Plate Park Slope (that blue cheese, though!), cured meats from Russo's Mozzarella & Pasta, and a demi baguette from Simple Loaf Bakehouse.

MOM COMES TO VISIT
BOARD

(SERVES 3-4)

When friends and family come to see us in New York City, one way our family welcomes them is with a board made with their palates in mind, waiting for them at the table. My mom is my best pal, and the kids and I are always giddy with excitement creating her board in anticipation of her arrival. When she arrives, the kids can't wait to share about all of the items over hugs and between bites.

SPRING VEGGIE BOARD

(SERVES 4-6)

Early on during the pandemic, I was lucky enough to be gifted Samin Nosrat's *Salt Fat Acid Heat*. The chapter on the power of salt was life changing for me. I experimented with blanching and salting for days in the kitchen, mesmerized by how the right combo of those two things could make vegetables out of this world delicious, more than my wildest dreams. This board is the result of that, the simplicity of well salted bounty from the earth.

BOARDS

- Valentine's Day Fondues
- Super Bowl Meatball Sliders
- St. Patrick's Day
- Fourth Of July Berry
- Thanksgiving Leftovers Sandwich
- Hannukah Latke
- Halloween
- Christmas

~5~

Holiday
Board Chapter

VALENTINE'S DAY SAVORY FONDUE BOARD

(SERVES 4-6)

Fondue is one of the best gifts given to the world by the 1960s. Sweet or savory, gimme a stick and I am down to dip. The perfect classic for a Valentine's Day gone well, here is our first of two fondue-meets-charcuterie boards, with a traditional cheese blend fondue base.

ON THE BOARD:

- 3 cups fondue cheese (see below)
- 2 cups andouille sausage
- 1 demi baguette, cubed
- 2 cups cherry tomatoes
- 2 cups mini tri color peppers
- 2 cups cauliflower
  (purple or green, if they have got it!)
- Parsley for garnish

FONDUE CHEESE RECIPE:

- ½ lb gruyere, finely grated
- ½ lb gouda, finely grated
- ¾ cup dry white wine
- 2 ½ tbsp corn starch
- 2 tbsp butter

Combine the cheeses and toss together with cornstarch in a bowl. Simmer butter and wine together in a saucepan over low heat. Slowly whisk in cheese in small amounts until smooth. Carefully pour into fondue serving bowl above flame on board.

PRESENTATION TIP:
Select a wide variety of colors. We like to blanch veggies like the cauliflower and carrots to make the colors pop!

idea

VALENTINE'S DAY
SWEET
FONDUE BOARD (SERVES 4-6)

The second offering of our fondue boards is perfect for that at-home date night, with a fluffy but still decadent chocolate dip.

ON THE BOARD:

- 2 cups sliced apples *(sweet and tart)*
- 2 cups strawberries
- 1 ½ cups raspberries
- 2 cups marshmallows
- 1 cup pretzels *(or something else salty)*
- 8-10 mini cinnamon rolls
  (or brownies, something that is for the over the top sweet-on-sweet folks, 2 pieces per person)

CHOCOLATE BASE RECIPE:

- 1 cup finely chopped good quality milk chocolate
- 1 cup finely chopped good quality semi sweet chocolate
- ¾ cup cream *(brought to room temperature)*
- ½ tbsp vanilla

Mix all ingredients over flame until smooth.

PRESENTATION TIP:
We recommend selecting an offering of both fruit and guilty pleasures for all palates and dietary desires.

SUPER BOWL MEATBALL SLIDERS BOARD (SERVES 6-8)

Our family LOVES football. So much so that the Super Bowl is its own holiday in our house. Meatball sliders (made with cheese crackers) are the perfect halftime grazing dinner.

ON THE BOARD:

- 6-8 mini hoagie rolls
- 8 slices provolone cheese, sliced in half and rolled
- 2 cups marinara sauce
- 1 cup grilled shishito peppers
- Fresh basil leaves
- Sliced onion and pickled mushrooms

CHEESE CRACKER MEATBALL SLIDERS RECIPE:

- 1 lb meatloaf mix
- ½ cup diced red onion
- 1 egg
- ½ cup milk
- ½ cup ground cheese crackers
- ¼ cup fresh parsley
- 3 cloves grated onion
- 1 tbsp Kosher salt
- ¼ cup grated parmesan cheese
- ½ cup all purpose flour

Preheat oven to 400 degrees. Mix all ingredients except flour with your hands. Take ¼ cup sized portions of mixture and roll into a ball. Coat in flour then place on a baking dish 1 inch apart. Bake for 18-20 minutes.

PRESENTATION TIP:
No time to make your own hoagie rolls? Buy store bought mini hoagies, and place cheddar cheese strips on top as football laces then top with everything bagel seasoning. Melt under broiler for 2-3 minutes.

ST. PATRICK'S DAY BOARD

(SERVES 6-8)

O ur annual Saint Paddy's board has one simple rule: It MUST have Irish soda bread (always from Amy's Bread in NYC) and cheeses. We use scooped out avocados for our four leaf clover design and fill with Irish cheddar dip.

FOURTH OF JULY BERRY BOARD

(SERVES 4-6)

Our muffin berry board has become a Fourth of July tradition. The best part? Muffins can be made the day before (or mini muffins can be store bought!), and on site assembly is easy as can be. A healthy brunch spin on the traditional flag cake dessert, this board is always a huge firework of a hit!

THANKSGIVING LEFTOVERS SANDWICH BOARD

(SERVES 6-8)

L et's face it, gorging on Thanksgiving leftovers is one of the best parts of the holiday! I like to put this board out around lunch time on Friday, and everyone makes their own plates. We always have more stashed away to replenish the board as needed for guests popping in throughout the day.

ON THE BOARD:

- Ramekins or one-cup sized bowls filled with your favorite side dishes *(Here we have sweet potato casserole, whipped butternut squash, green beans with fried onions, stuffing, and cranberry sauce)*
- ½ cup gravy
- ½ cup whole grain mustard
- 1 cup Brussels sprouts for that lettuce crunch
- ½ cup shredded or sliced carrots
- 2 cups shredded white and dark turkey meat
- ½ lb provolone cheese
- Dinner rolls or focaccia, cut into sandwich bread-sized pieces

PRESENTATION TIP:

Next to this board on the counter, we leave bags of chips and popcorn (our favorite snack!) and all the condiments so everyone can make the ultimate leftover sammy. For the grown ups, we also have a mimosa station to make your own, just the way you want it!

HANNUKAH LATKE BOARD

(SERVES 4-6)

A tradition we look forward to around the holidays is making our own latkes. Everyone pitches in, and we spend a day seeking out where to get lox in New York City, and everyone pitches in grating and frying up the potatoes (Yukon Golds, ALWAYS!). Capers, applesauce, sour cream and smoked fish dip are all key components to this board that we love to share with friends.

ON THE BOARD:

- 16-20 homemade mini latkes
- 3 mini cucumbers, sliced
- 1 cup cherry tomatoes
- ½ cup carrots
- ½ cup arugula
- ½ cup fresh dill
- 1 cup applesauce
- 1 cup sour cream
- 2 cups whitefish salad

MINI LATKES RECIPE:

- 4 Yukon Gold potatoes, peeled
- 1 small to medium red onion
- ⅓ cup all-purpose flour
- 1 ½ tsp baking powder
- ¼ cup parsley
- 1 egg
- 3 tsp Kosher salt
- Vegetable oil *(enough for ½ inch in the frying pan)*

Grate potatoes and onion, and wrap tightly in paper towels to drain water for 30 minutes. Heat oil to sizzle point. While oil is heating up, mix potato/onions with remaining ingredients. Using your hands is super fun at this point! Measure out ¼ cup balls of the latke mixture, then flatten with your hands and fry until a beautiful golden shade. It takes about 4 mins per side. Then rest on paper towels to drain and cool.

PRESENTATION TIP:

We make our latkes mini for tiny hands and to put as much as possible on the board. Think appetizer sizes with entrée portions! You can always make extra for a hungry crowd and replenish the board (or eat yourself with coffee the next day, like I do... Don't tell a soul, ok?).

HALLOWEEN BOARDS

Halloween is a month long affair in our house. The first week of October, we decorate the house with cobwebs and skeleton portraits, and we each pick out our costumes for the year. Every weekend is a party with a different haunting theme.

SKULL BROWNIE & CUPCAKE BOARD

(SERVES 8-10)

Our Halloween dessert board is always a crowd pleaser with kids and grown-ups alike, with substantial dessert sized options in two different flavors. Our skull pan was purchased at a baking and craft store and is the perfect wow treat for both Halloween and a pirate themed birthday party.

ON THE BOARD:

- 6-8 skull brownies
- 8-10 vanilla pumpkin cupcakes with buttercream frosting *(can be homemade or store bought for ease!)*
- 1 bag candy corn mix

SKULL BROWNIES RECIPE:

- 1 box brownie batter mix
  (we actually prefer baking mixes for this!)
- ½ cup Halloween themed sprinkles
  (orange and purple)

Spray skull pan thoroughly with cooking spray or butter. Pour 1 tbsp of sprinkles in one layer into pan molds. Mix remaining sprinkles into batter, then evenly distribute batter into molds. Bake 3-5 minutes more than recommended time to guarantee solidification of brownies into mold. Pop out when cool.

PRESENTATION TIP:
I always keep a bag or two of candy corn around the house during Halloween to use as a pop of color and texture on themed dessert/candy boards.

HALLOWEEN MOVIE NIGHT BOARDS

(SERVES 4-6)

Saturday night's alright for...holiday movie night! We love making a day of our themed movie adventures, especially when it comes to classic Halloween flicks. We start our day with character inspired pancakes with lots of fruit, and then spend the afternoon making treats for our epic movie viewing party board to be displayed and devoured during the showing that evening.

WITCHY QUESADILLA BOARD

(SERVES 4-6)

This Halloween brunch board is a perfect one to get the kids involved. Using tortillas for quesadillas or grilled cheese, all you need are some themed cookie cutters to bring this lunch to life!

ON THE BOARD:

- 1 family size bag tortilla chips, orange and black (*or blue corn*)
- 2 cups rice
- 1 cup sour cream
- 2 cups salsa
- 2 cups pinto or black beans
- 6 quesadillas or grilled cheese sandwiches on thin sandwich bread

After grilling the quesadillas or sandwiches, let cool on counter top for 5 minutes. Then, help little ones press Halloween cookie cutter shapes into quesadillas or sandwiches for witchy shapes. Place cut outs on top of tortilla chips and replenish on board as needed.

PRESENTATION TIP:
Let the kids pick which cookie cutters to use to make their own Halloween themes—ghosts, spiders, monsters, the sky is the spooky limit! My kids think I am a witch (Don't tell anyone my secret!) so we went with all things witch for ours.

SPOOKY SPIDER DIP BOARD

(SERVES 8-10)

Perfect for Halloween party hors d'œuvres, my nana's green onion dip can't be beat! Combine 4 cups full fat plain Greek yogurt, 1 tbsp garlic powder, 3 tsp kosher salt, 1 tbsp onion powder, and 3 tbsp fresh chopped green onion. Serve!

SCARECUTERIE TRICK OR TREAT BOARD

(SERVES 8-10)

Wow your Halloween guests with treats overload! We love finding individual vessels, like these paper coffins sold to put silverware in for parties, and filling them with customized surprises. We covered them and opened the coffins for the big reveal. A trick and then a treat! This creepy offering is topped off with monsters made with macarons and edible "googly" eyes and white chocolate molded witch hats. Our audience choice award goes to Lillypops, which come in a variety of colors and seasonal flavors.

CHRISTMAS BOARDS

ecember is my favorite time to be a New Yorker. Holiday lights line the streets, the Rockefeller Christmas tree welcomes folks to Manhattan, and the bliss (and sometimes drama!) of connecting with loved ones takes precedence over work spreadsheet stresses.

It is the time for making nana's recipes (along with happy messes!) in the kitchen with the kids... seeing the childhood delight in their eyes when setting silly Christmas pancakes down in front of them at the table... catching up with friends both new and old over a glass of wine and a plate of really, really (I mean really) good cheese. Yes, there is no place like home for the holidays. Especially when home is the Big Apple.

ROSEMARY WREATH CHARCUTERIE BOARD

(SERVES 8-10)

During the holidays, our front door is a rotation of yule tide cheer with visits from friends and family. I reserve a corner in my fridge for store bought cheery delectables to be able to easily welcome spontaneous guests, both kids and kids at heart, into our home on the fly. We pop open a bottle of Beaujolais wine (or bubbly!) and arrange our charcuterie spread with guests pitching in. Everyone has a job, and a glass!

ON THE BOARD:

- 3 packages rosemary sprigs
  (or sprigs cut from a rosemary Christmas tree, see below)
- 1 package raspberries or other red fruit
- 1 package blueberries or other dark hued fruit
- 1 cup pomegranate seeds
- Assorted cheeses in various shapes, including a round selection & triangle sliced Parmesan
- ½ lb assorted dried meats
- 1 cup olives
- ½ cup sun dried tomatoes
- 1 cup artichoke hearts or bread-and-butter pickles

Start with three ramekins around your board and place thin rosemary sprigs around the ramekins, molding into a circle pattern. Fill in other board ingredients around the rosemary and gently lift ramekins off the board. Fill each center of rosemary "wreath" circles with fruit and cheese items, as shown. Top each wreath with two triangle wedges and a small piece of fruit as bows.

PRESENTATION TIP:
We love the visual and comforting scent of having a rosemary "tree" in our kitchen during December. These can be purchased at the grocery store or a nursery. We pluck stems from the back of the tree, and use the front for homemade holiday decorations. We always buy more than one, and leave the others on friends' doorsteps with a handwritten card from the kiddos to spread the cheer.

HOLIDAY COOKIE DECORATING BOARD

(SERVES 6-8)

Holiday cookie decorating is a family tradition that dates back to my mom and nana in the kitchen with me as a tiny human, trying to not get caught with my fingers in the frosting! Every year, we decorate Christmas cookies to give as holiday presents. The kids are involved in every step, from baking... to decorating... to eating! We love to make this a neighborhood party, too. We often bake dozens of batches for kids to come over and join the fun, then take a box back home to their families.

TIP:
For friends who can't join, create a cookie decorating kit to go! In a container with a lid, place 10 sugar cookies, one tub of frosting, and bags of 1 cup portions of decorating items (sprinkles, candy canes and chocolate candies), then give!

CHRISTMAS WAFFLE BREAKFAST BOARD

(SERVES 4-6)

We have a blast with holiday themed weekend breakfasts leading up to the big day in December. This red velvet and vanilla waffle board was a treat to make, especially with Santa watching over the children! The same look can be created with dividing the waffle batter into two bowls, and mixing six drops of red food coloring into one.

INDEX

THANK YOU TO...

Maddy, Colton & Emmy for living this book with me.

Debbie Harmon, my mom, for showing me how to give others the gift of joy by making every day special. From hand drawn cards in my lunch box to baking giant cookies to dance parties as a kid, I hope I am half the mom you are.

Steve Dozier, my dad, for showing me at a young age to try all the things, take all the chances, and that food is an expression of life.

Laura Dozier for your support and keen eye.

My sister Katherine Dozier Moshman for all of the childhood memories that have turned into traditions noted in this book.

My sister Lee Dozier for sharing the moon with me.

Lindsey Isaacson for twenty plus years of always being up for an adventure and for teaching me how to give myself permission to enjoy happiness in little moments.

Mark Shacket for holding my hand during the wild ride that became creating this book.

Our incredible designer Manuel González Ruiz, I am grateful to you and your artistry beyond words.

My dear friend Michel Hausmann for the idea that Manuel and I should collaborate on this book.

Garrett King for your friendship, eating a lot of these boards with the kids and me, and for the idea of this book's name.

Joe Trentacosta, the brother I never had, for being such an important part of getting BOARD AF into the world alongside Holly Garman.

Kristen Piazza for seeing the potential in my stay-at-home hobby.

The incredible team at LDK Productions: Michael Shannon, Amanda Nicastro & Logan Dewitt, for supporting me while this book was created.

All of my friends and family who connected with me during the pandemic over the food boards.

And to YOU, dear reader, for joining us on this BOARD AF journey.

Photography by: **Russ Rowland**

Lisa Dozier is a food enthusiast living in Brooklyn NY with her three amazing kiddos and their puppy, Georgia. Maddy, 10, Colton, 5, and Emmy, 5, all love to get in the kitchen with her to help make (and eat) board creations. In addition to all things home cookin' charcuterie, Lisa is also a theatre producer and manager, wanderluster, and collector of vintage fashion.

NOTES

This first edition of 2000 copies was baked, bound, and printed by Artes Gráficas Palermo in Madrid, Spain. Cooked up with IBM Plex Serif, IBM Plex Sans & FFF Tusji fonts. November 2021.